SCIENCE DISCOVERY

Ecosystems

Q&A

Gillian Richardson

MEDIA ENHANCED BOOKS
AV2 BY WEIGL
ADDED VALUE • AUDIO VISUAL

www.av2books.com

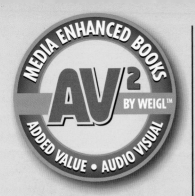

AV² provides enriched content that supplements and complements this book. Weigl's AV² books strive to create inspired learning and engage young minds in a total learning experience.

Your AV² Media Enhanced books come alive with...

 Audio
Listen to sections of the book read aloud.

 Key Words
Study vocabulary, and complete a matching word activity.

 Video
Watch informative video clips.

 Quizzes
Test your knowledge.

 Embedded Weblinks
Gain additional information for research.

 Slide Show
View images and captions, and prepare a presentation.

 Try This!
Complete activities and hands-on experiments.

... and much, much more!

Go to **www.av2books.com**, and enter this book's unique code.

BOOK CODE

D 5 0 8 3 4 5

AV² by Weigl brings you media enhanced books that support active learning.

Published by AV² by Weigl
350 5th Avenue, 59th Floor
New York, NY 10118
Website: www.av2books.com   www.weigl.com

Library of Congress Control Number: 2013942901
ISBN 978-1-62127-413-1 (hard cover)
ISBN 978-1-62127-419-3 (soft cover)

Printed in the United States of America, in North Mankato, Minnesota
1 2 3 4 5 6 7 8 9 0 17 16 15 14 13

062013
WEP040413B

Editor Aaron Carr
Designer Mandy Christiansen

Every reasonable effort has been made to trace ownership and to obtain permission to reprint copyright material. The publishers would be pleased to have any errors or omissions brought to their attention so that they may be corrected in subsequent printings.

Photo Credits
Weigl acknowledges Getty Images as its primary photo supplier for this title.

Contents

What Is an Ecosystem?

A community of living things that share a **habitat** is called an ecosystem. However, to fully understand what an ecosystem is, scientists must take a closer look at the subject. Scientists have to ask more questions, such as what kinds of ecosystems are there, where are they found, and what kinds of **organisms** do they support? By thinking about the problem and asking questions, they can gain a better understanding of ecosystems.

How Scientists Use Inquiry to Answer Questions

When scientists try to answer a question, they follow the process of scientific inquiry. They begin by making observations and asking questions. They then propose an answer to their question. This is called the hypothesis. The hypothesis guides scientists as they research the issue. Research can involve performing experiments or reading books on the subject. When their research is finished, scientists examine their results and review their hypothesis. Often, they discover that their hypothesis was incorrect. If this happens, they revise their hypothesis and go through the process of scientific inquiry again.

Process of Scientific Inquiry

Observation

Ecosystems are made up of many organisms living together in a habitat. There are, however, many types of organisms and habitats. So what exactly is an ecosystem?

Have You Answered the Question?

The cycle of scientific inquiry never truly ends. For example, once scientists know how sea otters affect an ecosystem, they may need to ask, "What do sea otters rely upon to survive?"

Research

Scientists study the sizes of ecosystems, their locations, and the living things that call them home. They do this by asking questions such as, "How do **species** relate to each other and their habitats?"

Results

Ecosystems are complex. For example, discovering how sea otters affect an ecosystem leads to more questions, more hypotheses, and more experiments.

Hypothesis

The variety of life across different ecosystems has led scientists to hypothesize that every species is adapted to its environment. From sea dragons to lynxes, all organisms in an ecosystem are interdependent.

Experiment

To test this hypothesis, scientists perform experiments, such as reintroducing wolves into Yellowstone National Park.

What Are the Major Ecosystems of the World?

Scientists have categorized all of Earth's environments into major ecosystems. The number of major ecosystems differs according to some scientists. In general, ecosystems can be classified as either land-based or **aquatic**. Similar ecosystems grouped together are called biomes. Biome types include desert, forest, and aquatic biomes.

Land-based ecosystems are sometimes named for their main plant species, which provide habitats for many living things. The type of plants and animals in an ecosystem depends on the climate, soil, and **elevation**. Aquatic ecosystems differ depending on a number of factors, such as whether they have fresh water or salt water, deep seas, or shallow reefs. Humans are also a factor. People can change the environment and create **artificial** habitats.

Aquatic Ecosystems

Inland Water
Location: Lakes, ponds, rivers, wetlands
Features: Still or flowing water, varied **biodiversity**, freshwater

Ocean
Location: Covers 71 percent of Earth
Features: Plants near the surface, varied animal life, saltwater

Land-based Ecosystems

Boreal Forest, or Taiga
Location: Areas with short summers located in the Far North
Features: Mainly **coniferous** and old-growth trees, furry animals, many birds

Desert
Location: Areas typically near the tropics or the North and South Poles
Features: Deeply rooted plants, few animals or birds, low rainfall, very hot or very cold

Grassland
Location: Bordering forest areas
Features: Natural grasses, herbivores, alternately dry and wet

Temperate Forest
Location: Areas with cold winters
Features: **Deciduous** trees, rich soil, limited number of species

Tropical Rainforest
Location: Near the equator
Features: Dense vegetation, high biodiversity, warm and wet

Tundra
Location: In mountains above the tree line, around Arctic polar region
Features: Low, shallow-rooted plants, cold permafrost, few animals

Digging Deeper

Your Challenge!

All ecosystems are linked. Ocean ecosystems touch land ecosystems. Land ecosystems are connected to each other. Each ecosystem affects the others. Learn more by researching how alpine, or mountain, regions affect desert regions. How are the two interconnected?

Summary

Ecosystems can be found in all parts of the world. Scientists organize Earth into major ecosystem types.

Further Inquiry

With so many different kinds of ecosystems, maybe we should ask:

Where are ecosystems found?

Where Are Ecosystems Found?

People might think that ecosystems are limited to certain places. This is only partly true. Some ecosystems, such as the taiga, may only be found in the northern regions of Earth. Others, such as deserts, may be found in many different places.

The Earth's geography and its climate systems limit where ecosystems may survive. The Earth is made up of ecosystems. Scientists refer to the collection of ecosystems on Earth as the biosphere.

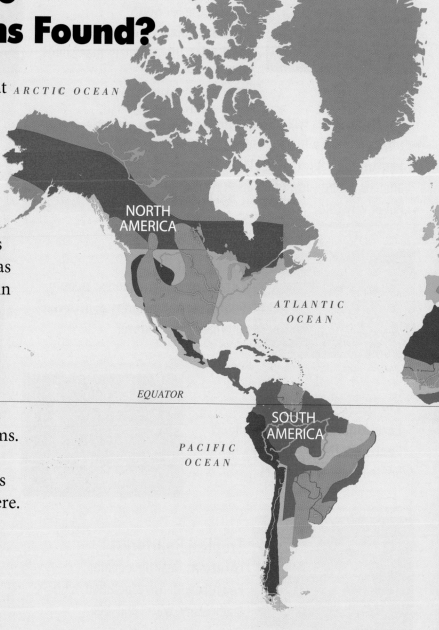

ARCTIC OCEAN

NORTH AMERICA

ATLANTIC OCEAN

EQUATOR

SOUTH AMERICA

PACIFIC OCEAN

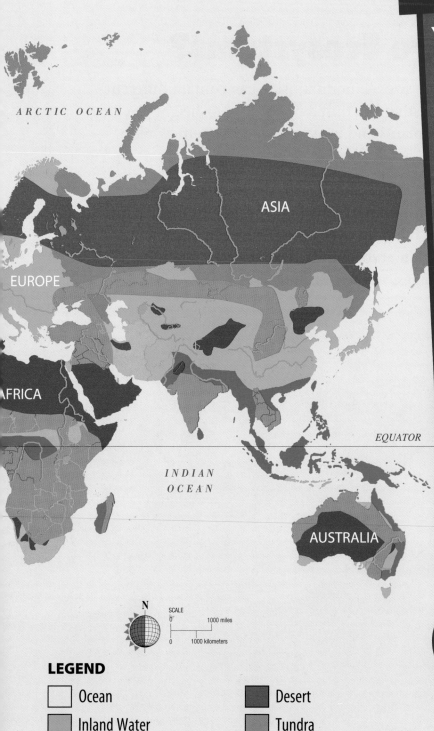

Digging Deeper

Your Challenge!

Explore the Taiga. How does this ecosystem affect the entire biosphere? Research the threats to this ecosystem and the steps scientists are taking to protect it. Write a report that summarizes your different findings.

Summary

Ecosystems may be classified into different types, and these types may be found all over the world. Some, like the taiga, may stretch all the way around the world. Other ecosystems may be small and may only occur in specific areas of the world.

Further Inquiry

The major ecosystems are often very large. Are all ecosystems large? Maybe we should ask:

How big are ecosystems?

ARCTIC OCEAN

ASIA

EUROPE

AFRICA

EQUATOR

INDIAN OCEAN

AUSTRALIA

N

SCALE

0   1000 miles

0   1000 kilometers

LEGEND

- Ocean
- Inland Water
- Tropical Rainforest
- Boreal Forest, or Taiga
- Desert
- Tundra
- Temperate Forest
- Grassland

How Big Are Ecosystems?

An ecosystem can be any size. A mountainside can contain different ecosystems, each one existing at a different altitude, or height. A cliff face that supports a few plants and insects is an ecosystem, while a vast desert is another. A cave is an ecosystem, too.

A coral reef is an ecosystem found in warm, shallow ocean water. It consists of colonies of tiny animals called polyps. Polyps make hard limestone skeletons that build up over time. These can become very large, providing a habitat for hundreds of species, including fish, sea anemones, sponges, sea horses, and turtles.

An ecosystem can be as small as a single drop of water. Tiny creatures called **microorganisms** live in these ecosystems. Here, tiny octopus-like animals called hydra hunt water fleas, and algae extract nutrients from the water around them. Even larger organisms, such as mosquito larvae, can live in a drop of water. No matter how big or how small, a healthy ecosystem is in perfect balance with itself.

▼ Cave ecosystems are home to many organisms that have adapted to life in this harsh environment.

Digging Deeper

Your Challenge!

Create your own ecosystem. To do so, first investigate how an artificial ecosystem works. Artificial ecosystems include aquariums, terrariums, and even zoos. Then, try to create your own. What elements will you need to include? How much of each element, such as water, is needed to keep the system in balance?

Summary

Ecosystems can be any size, from a drop of water to entire mountain ranges. Each ecosystem is different.

Further Inquiry

With such a variety of ecosystems, in both kind and in size, maybe we should ask:

What lives in an ecosystem?

Q&A

What Lives In an Ecosystem?

Many kinds of living things inhabit ecosystems. Scientists refer to living things collectively as organisms. Plants, animals, insects, even tiny bacteria, are organisms. Every organism follows a life cycle. It is born, it grows, it reproduces, and it eventually dies. Then, the new generation experiences the life cycle.

Life can be found in almost every place on Earth. Organisms can thrive in almost any environment, even the most extreme. Some live near vents, or holes, on the ocean floor. These vents release very hot, poisonous gases from the center of Earth. The organisms that live here have adapted to survive such harsh conditions. Others live inside dark caves. Living in the dark, they do not need to see, so they have adapted to life with no eyes.

⌄ Blue whales are dependent upon tiny shrimp-like creatures called krill.

Organisms range in size from creatures that are microscopic to gigantic whales and redwood trees. Some species exist in numbers too large to count. Others may dwindle to a few individuals or disappear completely and so become **extinct**.

A daisy and a blue whale are both organisms. Though the daisy and the whale are both alive, they are very different from each other. Scientists have developed a system, called classification, that sorts organisms based on their differences and similarities. One type of classification is called a kingdom. There are currently 5 kingdoms. Of these, the plant kingdom and the animal kingdom are the most familiar to people. A third contains such things as mushrooms and other fungi. The other two contain microscopic, simple creatures.

How Many Organisms Are There?

Scientists discover new organisms daily. With each discovery, they must use the method of inquiry to determine if it is a new species. They must ask questions about it, form a hypothesis, study it, and test it. Over the past few decades alone, scientists have identified more than 1,300 new species, including a new kind of bird-eating spider and the tube-nosed fruit bat. Each new discovery expands scientific understanding and teaches people more about just how complex ecosystems are. These discoveries also lead to new questions.

With each new discovery, scientists revise the number of organisms they believe exist on Earth. Currently, they estimate that there are about 8.8 million different species. They have only classified a small number of these, about 1.8 million. Scientists think they have identified most birds, flowering plants, and large mammals, but smaller creatures, such as **invertebrates**, exist in staggering numbers. It is possible that there are more than 30 million invertebrate species.

This wide variety of life developed over long periods of time. Organisms particularly suited to a certain **niche** survived to pass along their traits to future generations, while organisms less suited died out. In other niches, organisms developed in different ways. This gradual process is called natural selection.

Natural selection has resulted in a multitude of organisms, all ideally suited to their different ecosystems. It may take millions of years for a new species to emerge, but natural selection is happening all the time.

> ❯ The leaf cutter ant adapted to its environment over millions of years. There are an estimated 22,000 ant species.

Digging Deeper

Your Challenge!

Go online and learn about the International Institute for Species Exploration (IISE). What do the scientists who work there do, and how do they do it? Create a chart listing their most recent discoveries and where on Earth they were found.

Summary

There are so many species in the biosphere, that it would be impossible for you to count them all.

Further Inquiry

To describe the variety of life in an ecosystem, scientists use the term biodiversity. What exactly do they mean by it? Maybe we should ask:

What is biodiversity?

⌃ Along with the tube-nosed fruit bat, scientists also discovered 24 new frog and almost 100 new insect species on the same expedition, or trip.

What Is Biodiversity?

An ecosystem contains a wide variety of life. Scientists call this variety biodiversity. Some ecosystems may contain more biodiversity than others. A coral reef has more biodiversity than a drop of pond water. Still, most ecosystems must have some biodiversity.

This biodiversity in an ecosystem develops over time. As the ecosystem evolves, each organism adapts to suit its environment. In one ecosystem, for example, ants may have adapted to nest in trees, while in another they may have adapted to nest underground. In turn, the organisms that feed on those ants, such as anteaters, also change to suit their environment. Over time, the tongues of anteaters evolved to reach deep into ant mounds so they could eat the ants.

❯ Some scientists recognize up to eight different subspecies of lion.

↑ Scientists differ on how many kinds of penguin there are, with numbers ranging from 16 to 20 different species.

Your Challenge!

Biodiversity developed in part when a species had to adapt to a new environment. Such adaptations can take millions of years. They can also happen relatively quickly. To learn more, research how scientists believe the polar bear developed from the brown bear. How long do they think this change took? Just how closely related are polar bears and brown bears today?

Summary

Biodiversity is the variety of organisms that inhabit an ecosystem. Biodiversity happens over time and leads to different kinds of species living in different ecosystems all over the world.

Subspecies may evolve when a species is spread out and lives in different areas. In this case, each population may change subtly over time. This creates even more biodiversity.

The biodiversity in nature improves people's lives. Humans value nature for its beauty and the enjoyment it brings. They create works of art using animals, birds, and flowers as subjects. People visit different places to see rare plant species or unusual wildlife. The diversity that nature offers helps people learn about the past, present, and future.

Further Inquiry

Biodiversity evolves over time, but maybe we should ask:

Why is biodiversity important?

Why Is Biodiversity Important?

With so much biodiversity on Earth, we might wonder why it matters if a species becomes extinct. After all, over millions of years, countless life forms have developed and disappeared. Yet life still goes on. Scientists, however, do not know how the disappearance of these species affected their respective ecosystems.

Biodiversity helps keep ecosystems in balance. Biodiversity can be thought of in terms of a set of dominoes, where each piece depends on another piece. When the first piece is pushed over, it can knock over the next, and so on. They all tumble over, one after another. Biodiversity can be similar. Remove one species, and it can greatly affect others.

Biodiversity is also important because human beings depend on animals and plants for food, and even medicine. Scientists can use the **genetic material** found in wild plants to make new crops that are easier to grow or that produce more food. About one quarter of all prescription medicines have ingredients that come from the natural world. With each extinct species, important diversity is lost forever, and with it potential benefits for humans.

> ❯ Ladybugs feed on the insects that live in a typical garden. Without the ladybug to keep their population in balance, these other insects could destroy the garden.

Digging Deeper

Your Challenge!

Research on the Internet and find examples of some plants that have been used to create new medicines for people. What kinds of medicines are they? What illnesses are they used to treat? Are there any problems associated with using these plants, such as the threat of habitat destruction from removing too many plants?

Summary

Biodiversity is one of the key factors that keeps an ecosystem balanced. Remove a single organism, and the entire ecosystem may be thrown off balance.

Further Inquiry

Biodiversity plays an important role in maintaining an ecosystem. Does anything else? Maybe we should ask:

Do ecosystems have basic needs?

Q&A

Do Ecosystems Have Basic Needs?

The eco in ecosystem comes from the ancient Greek word *oikos*, which means "house." In English, eco can mean "the place where things live—their environment or habitat." For an ecosystem to support life, it must provide a habitat, and a habitat must contain key resources: food, water, shelter, and living space. Organisms cannot survive without these things.

Plants change sunlight, water, and carbon dioxide into food during a process called photosynthesis. They use this food to grow flowers, fruit, leaves, and roots. The fruit contains seeds, which will become the next generation of the plant.

Numerous animals eat plants. They do so to nourish their bodies so they can grow, repair injuries, and produce young.

Photosynthesis of Plants

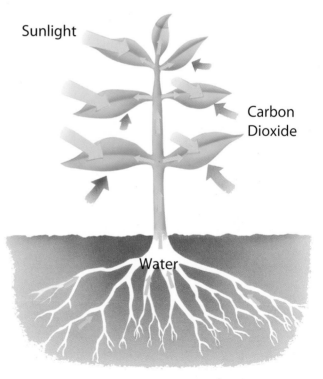

Sunlight

Carbon Dioxide

Water

⌃ Plant growth depends on the amount of sun, and the water and nutrients in the soil.

Living space is important for both animals and plants. In crowded conditions, plant roots cannot develop properly. Fast-growing plants can out-compete slower growing plants for resources. Animals may not have enough food for all members of an ecosystem. Where there are limited resources, there also will be a limit to the organisms able to live there, both in kind and number.

⌄ In some ecosystems with limited resources, a single brown bear may need up to 950 square miles (2,500 square kilometers) of living space.

Digging Deeper

Your Challenge!

The basic elements of an ecosystem are all interconnected. Learn more by researching the relationship between vegetation, soil quality, and the water cycle in an ecosystem.

Summary

Ecosystems must be able to support organisms by providing adequate food, water, shelter, and living space. Without these things, organisms cannot survive.

Further Inquiry

With all of these requirements, from biodiversity to basic needs such as water and food, maybe we should ask:

How does an ecosystem work?

How Does an Ecosystem Work?

An ideal ecosystem runs like a finely tuned machine, with each part depending on the rest. A single change can affect the whole system. If the balance is changed in an ecosystem, it can have major effects on all of the individual parts.

Trees use water and the nutrients in the soil to grow. Various animals use the trees. Some spend their entire lives in trees. Birds shelter in holes in tree trunks or build nests among branches. They might feed on insects living in the same tree, helping to prevent damage to its leaves or bark. Some insects **pollinate** a tree's flowers so that fruit or seeds will be produced.

When a tree dies, it begins to break down. Fungi, such as mushrooms, and insects help this process. The nutrients from the tree are returned to the soil, and then feed the next generation of trees.

The more biodiversity an ecosystem has, the more links there are between its inhabitants. Scientists investigate the cycles in nature to understand what keeps things in balance. Science can help provide the tools to restore order when something goes wrong, usually because of human action.

Digging Deeper

Your Challenge!

Construct your own balanced ecosystem. Choose an ecosystem, such as a forest or a pond. Research what kinds of organisms inhabit this ecosystem and what their different needs are. Then create a chart showing how the organisms interact with each other and how the ecosystem would be affected if one organism were removed.

Summary

An ecosystem works like a machine. Each part is necessary in order for the whole system to work.

Further Inquiry

Healthy ecosystems are in balance, but do they always stay that way? Maybe we should ask:

Can ecosystems change?

❮ Woodpeckers have evolved a number of adaptations in their heads to prevent brain damage from the repeated impact of their bills against trees.

Can Ecosystems Change?

Natural changes to the environment occur constantly. Some happen slowly, and it may take a long time before humans can see the effects. Gradual changes in temperature or rainfall amounts may mean fewer plants can grow. Less vegetation means less food and shelter for animals. They must adapt, move to other areas, or die out. Other organisms that are better suited may move in.

Other kinds of changes, such as natural disasters, can suddenly disrupt an environment. An example of a sudden change in an environment took place in May 1980, when Mount St. Helens erupted in the state of Washington.

This eruption gave scientists a chance to study what happens to an ecosystem when it undergoes a sudden and violent change. Some hypothesized that life would be wiped out and the mountain would remain forever barren and deserted.

The volcanic blast threw thick clouds of ash miles into the air and devastated 230 square miles (595 sq. km) of forest. Plant life was scorched or buried. Most small mammals were killed immediately or died later because their food, water, and shelter were gone.

Yet some coniferous trees survived because they were protected by late spring snow. They spread their seeds quickly. Roots from burned plants soon created new growth. Scientists found that as plant life gradually returned, animals moved back to the region. The area was able to stabilize over time, and animal and plant life adapted to the new conditions. Scientists revised their hypotheses and learned much from the event.

˅ Scientists have been amazed at how quickly the ecosystem of Mount St. Helens is recovering.

Digging Deeper

Your Challenge!

Sometimes ecosystems change when a new species is introduced by accident. Such a species is called an invasive species. Invasive species almost always have a negative effect on their new ecosystem. Learn more by researching the brown tree snake, which was accidentally introduced to the island of Guam. What effect has the snake had on that island's ecosystem?

Summary

Ecosystems are changing constantly, whether from natural forces or human influence. These changes can occur slowly or quickly.

Further Inquiry

Since species are dependent on each other, often for food, maybe we should ask:

What is a food chain?

What Is a Food Chain?

All living things need food for energy. This need links them together like a chain. Each organism occupies its own niche in a food chain. Plants and algae are often the first link on a food chain. They are called producers because they are able to convert the Sun's energy into a form that animals can use. Animals known as primary consumers eat plants. Other animals called secondary consumers eat these animals. Tertiary consumers are at the top of a food chain. When producers and consumers die, another important member of the food chain, the decomposers, breaks down their tissues.

A food chain in the Arctic might begin with microscopic ocean plants called phytoplankton. These tiny organisms take the nutrients they need from the sun and the sea. Phytoplankton are eaten by sea-dwelling creatures, such as copepods, tiny relatives of lobsters and crabs. Shrimps called krill eat the copepods. Krill is a favorite food of seals, which are eaten by polar bears.

The polar bear is at the top of its food chain, meaning that it has no natural enemies. When a polar bear dies, scavengers and bacteria will consume its body. It will be changed into nutrients. These will be washed back into the sea where they will be used by phytoplankton. The food chain has come full circle.

Food chains interact. Not only polar bears eat seals. Killer whales eat them, too. They form another food chain. The biodiversity in an ecosystem allows for a series of food chains. Each chain connects to another, forming a food web.

Tertiary
Consumers

Secondary
Consumers

Primary
Consumers

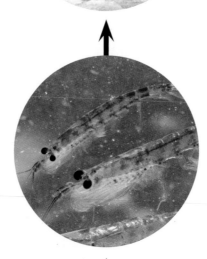

Producers

Digging Deeper

Your Challenge!

Individual food chains join to make food webs. Research the different organisms that make the food web on the African savannah. Then, create a chart that illustrates this food web. Predict the effect on the ecosystem if one of the organisms were removed from the food web. What organisms would be directly affected?

Summary

The food chain is the natural cycle that sees organisms dependent on each other for food.

Further Inquiry

How do different animal populations stay balanced? Maybe we should ask:

What is a population cycle?

What Is a Population Cycle?

A cycle is the orderly way events occur in nature. In a cycle, the end of the process leads back to the starting point, much like a circle. Some animals are so closely linked on a food chain that their population increases and decreases in a regular cycle. Scientists have learned that the lynx and its main prey, the snowshoe hare, follow this kind of population cycle.

Over a period of nine to ten years, hares in a community produce enormous numbers of offspring. This makes hunting easy for the lynx. Soon, the lynx eat so many hares that the number of hares drops. With less of their favorite food available, the number of lynx also drops. When the population of this predator declines, populations of hare begin to rise again. This increase is followed closely by an increase in the lynx population. These cycles continue, and the ecosystem stays in a balanced state.

❯ A lynx may consume more than 200 hares in a year.

▲ The snowshoe hare's fur changes from brown to white in the winter. This change can take up to 10 weeks.

Digging Deeper

Your Challenge!

Use a library or go online and research the population cycle of the snowshoe hare and the lynx over the last 100 years. Make a graph of these numbers, and then try to predict the next five high and low points of the cycle.

Summary

A population cycle is the regular rise and fall of one species in an ecosystem. It may cause a similar rise and fall in the population of interdependent species.

Further Inquiry

The lynx and hare relationship shows how important one species can be to another. Are some species important not just to one other species, but to entire ecosystems? Maybe we should ask:

What is a keystone species?

Q&A

What Is a Keystone Species?

While all species in a habitat depend on other species for survival, some species play a more important role in maintaining the quality of the habitat than others. These important species are called keystone species, and if they disappear from a habitat, the connection between other species in the habitat will begin to change. The delicately balanced ecosystem may fall apart.

Scientists hypothesized that the California sea otter was a keystone species. This otter is a West Coast mammal that lives on floating kelp beds. Its main food is spiny sea urchins from the ocean floor. Prized for its fur, the sea otter was hunted in the 1700–1800s until it was believed to be extinct.

⌄ At the population's lowest point, it is estimated there were only 1,000 to 2,000 sea otters left in the world.

Since otters were no longer eating sea urchins, the sea urchin population grew. The urchins ate kelp until it, too, was gone. Kelp beds provided a spawning, or mating, place for certain fish. With the kelp gone, these fish had no place to spawn and they began to die off. Kelp also softened the force of waves, which kept the shore from eroding, or washing away, during storms. With the otters gone, the ecosystem was thrown off-balance.

Scientists hypothesized that by reintroducing the sea otter balance could be restored. In the 1960s and 1970s, sea otters from Alaska were brought south to the Pacific coast. Protected from hunting, the otters thrived. Sea urchins had a predator once again. As sea urchin numbers fell, the kelp began to grow. The fish had their spawning ground back. The scientists' hypothesis had been proved correct.

Digging Deeper

Your Challenge!

Removing certain species from an ecosystem can have unforeseen consequences. To learn more, research the history of the American alligator. How did scientists determine it was a keystone species? What other species were directly affected by the alligator's removal?

Summary

A keystone species has a larger effect on maintaining an ecosystem's balance than other species. Remove it, and an entire ecosystem will become unbalanced.

Further Inquiry

Each species depends on others, but what happens if one species becomes extinct? Maybe we should ask:

How long can a species survive?

How Long Can a Species Survive?

Scientists believe that since life began on Earth, more than 99 percent of all species that have ever lived have gone extinct. Even now, they estimate that species are disappearing at a rate of about 50 to 135 species per day. In part, natural selection is responsible for how long a species may last. A species' ability to adapt to new environments is also very important. If a species cannot adapt, it may not survive.

A species may be at risk if it is overly dependent on one resource. For example, the monarch butterfly is at risk in some areas. It lays its eggs on the milkweed plant, the only plant species monarch larvae can eat. Habitat loss has caused a decrease in milkweed in parts of North America, also decreasing monarch populations.

Around the world, many old-growth forests are threatened by deforestation, or the destruction of forested areas.

Dependence on a specific ecosystem can also put a species at risk. An old-growth forest is a mature, complex, and diverse forest community. It is made up of birds, herbs, insects, mammals, shrubs, and trees. A seabird called the marbled murrelet nests in old-growth forests, mainly near the west coast of Canada. Logging has disrupted this habitat. Some people are trying to preserve the remaining old-growth forests in order to save the murrelet.

❯ The marbled murrelet forages for food near the ocean shore before returning to its nest.

Digging Deeper

Your Challenge!

One of the great mass extinctions of the world occurred in North America at the end of the last ice age, more than 10,000 years ago. Create a poster with drawings or pictures of the kinds of animals that went extinct during this period. How many species went extinct? What do scientists hypothesize was the reason?

Summary

Natural selection and a species' ability to adapt play very important roles in determining how long a species may last.

Further Inquiry

Humans have adapted to almost every environment on Earth. Humans can also be very destructive. To understand our place in the biosphere, maybe we should ask:

How do humans affect ecosystems?

How Do Humans Affect Ecosystems?

Humans share the same basic needs with other organisms. They need food, water, shelter, and living space. Yet humans have the ability to change ecosystems more than any other species. They can change entire landscapes in order to farm the food they need. They can dam rivers to create vast water supplies.

This ability has allowed humans to spread all over the earth. Humans have lived in the frozen Arctic, high in the mountains, and even in outer space. For this reason, human activity has been responsible for many harmful changes to the environment. Roads and houses affect the ecosystems on which they are built. Logging and mining can upset the environment. The destruction of natural habitats caused by human activity is a leading cause of the loss of biodiversity. Many species have become extinct due to human activity.

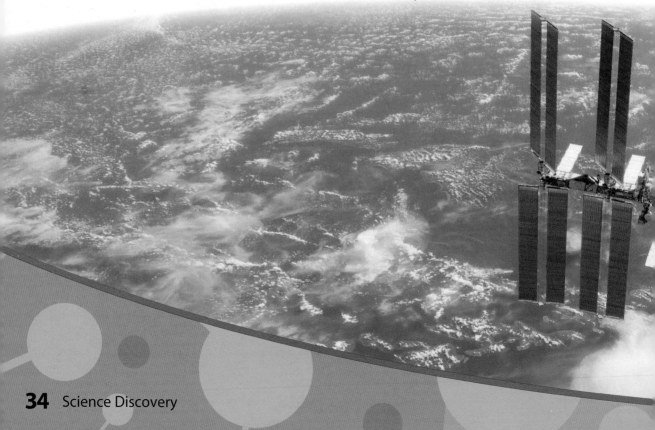

Human use of **fossil fuels**, such as coal, oil, and gas, has led to air pollution, causing a worldwide problem known as global warming. Scientists have shown that Earth's temperature is increasing. If this continues, they hypothesize that major environmental changes could occur. Melting polar icecaps could cause coastal areas to flood. Weather patterns may become unpredictable, bringing more destructive storms.

As science helps people understand the effect they can have on both the local and global ecosystem, people can begin to make the necessary changes to the ways they behave.

⌄ From fresh air to drinking water, scientists designed the International Space Station like an ecosystem, providing for the needs of the astronauts on board.

Can Endangered Species Be Saved?

Thousands of species around the world are endangered. With the help of science, these organisms can sometimes be saved.

Wolves were once common in Yellowstone National Park. By the 1930s, hunting and other human activities had wiped out these animals in the western United States.

In 1995, scientists trapped 14 wolves from different packs in Canada. They brought these wolves to Yellowstone, where they were slowly introduced to their new environment. The wolves were kept separately in large pens. The scientists studied their individual behaviors, and the wolves eventually were placed together in packs.

Studying the wolves before releasing them resulted in almost all the packs making a successful transition to life in Yellowstone National Park. Scientists have been able to repeat this success with other species in other locations.

❯ By 2011, scientists estimated that the number of wolves in Yellowstone had increased to 98. In recent years, this number has decreased, partly due to wolves being killed when they leave the protection of the park.

Digging Deeper

Your Challenge!

Research how many endangered species there are in the world. Create a chart that lists the number of endangered species by continent or country. How many are there in Asia? North America? The United States? Which country has the most endangered species?

Summary

In some cases, science can help save endangered species. The general public must be supportive.

Further Inquiry

To help save species and their environments, many people are now trying to be more eco-friendly when they travel. Maybe we should ask:

What is ecotourism?

What Is Ecotourism?

People often enjoy visiting places of natural beauty. For those people who live in such areas, these visitors have become an important source of income. Resorts and campsites may be built for tourists. Trails may be cut through forests. These activities change the natural landscape, contribute to pollution, and disrupt animal and plant life.

Over time, people recognized the problems tourism caused. They began to develop a new way of traveling called ecotourism. Ecotourism is defined by The International Ecotourism Society (TIES) as "responsible travel to natural areas that conserves the environment and sustains the well-being of local people." Often, the money brought to such areas by ecotourists helps support the endangered ecosystems.

❯ Snorkeling with humpback whales is a popular activity in some areas, though it can stress the whale.

Ecotourists can take a boat tour to see whales during their migration along the west coast of North America. They can also go on safaris in an African wildlife preserve, where animals such as elephants and lions are protected from hunters.

The whooping crane is one example of how ecotourism has helped a species. This bird spends its winters at a refuge on the coast of Texas. The presence of the cranes draws many tourists to the area. Money from these visitors helps support the cranes' habitat.

The rain forests of Costa Rica in Central America are another ecotourism destination. Visitors spend millions of dollars each year viewing Costa Rican ecosystems. There are rules about where tourists can go and how they should act to help preserve the rain forests.

Digging Deeper

Your Challenge!

Despite best efforts, ecotourism still can have negative effects. Identify the dangers for the whales that are involved in whale watching. Evaluate the idea of ecotourism and whale watching. Debate the issue with a friend or in class. Take a side, either for or against whale watching.

Summary

Ecotourism is a way of enjoying nature while having as little impact on the ecosystem as possible.

Further Inquiry

National parks are often praised as examples of ecotourism that work for both people and the environment. Maybe we should ask:

Are national parks for people or animals?

Are National Parks for People or Animals?

National parks are some of the only places where larger animals can still live in nearly natural conditions. These parks are some of the best places for people to see animals in nature.

National parks are natural areas that are protected by the government. There are more than 50 national parks in the United States. Visitors must follow a set of rules that protect both people and the natural environment. For example, they are not allowed to remove anything from the parks. They must also pay a fee to enter. This helps with the costs of protecting and preserving the parks.

Many people want more roads built in the parks. They want to reach remote areas to view wildlife and participate in recreational activities such as camping. Others support mining and logging in parks to take advantage of **natural resources**.

↑ Yellowstone's bison often travel along the park's roads, making for dangerous situations with people.

Digging Deeper

Your Challenge!

National parks are not favored by everyone. Learn more about the issue by researching the history of the national park system in the United States. Write a report either defending the idea of national parks, or in favor of disbanding them.

Summary

National parks strive to balance the protection of natural ecosystems with the desire of people to enjoy them.

Further Inquiry

Fully understanding ecosystems has involved asking many questions and researching many issues. Taking all we have learned, maybe we can finally answer:

What is an ecosystem?

Putting It All Together

An ecosystem is the community of organisms that share a habitat. Ecosystems can be any size, from a drop of water to a vast desert. The Earth is composed of different ecosystems, collectively called the biosphere. In these systems live countless kinds of organisms. This variety is called biodiversity, and it is necessary for most ecosystems to survive and thrive.

All organisms are interconnected, and a healthy ecosystem functions when every organism can play its part, sometimes acting as food for other members of the system. These relationships form food chains. Many food chains connect to form a food web. Some species in an ecosystem are more important. They are keystones, and their removal can destroy the balance of an entire system.

Where People Fit In

Human activity has been the cause of much ecosystem disruption. People are beginning to realize, not only the effect they have on nature, but that they are connected to it, too. National parks and ecotourism have allowed people to save entire environments, and even bring endangered species back from the brink of extinction.

Science and the process of scientific inquiry allows people to study and understand ecosystems. This helps people understand their own place on Earth, the great ecosystem that sustains everyone. The more people learn about how ecosystems work, the more questions arise.

❮ The often colorful biodiversity in nature is the product of millions of years of evolution and adaptation.

Eco-Careers

Conservation Officer

A conservation officer's job is to help protect and preserve natural resources, such as wildlife. A key role of a conservation officer is to enforce laws that people who hunt and fish must obey. They also may protect the public from dangerous wildlife that has entered an urban area, such as a bear looking for food in a backyard.

A conservation officer learns a great deal about wildlife and may assist biologists in the protection of animals. Sometimes, the officer might also be asked to speak to groups interested in the outdoors.

Biologist

Biologists often work outdoors. They may work in nature, or in a nature center or zoo. They also carry out experiments in a lab, or work with museums to help create realistic displays.

Often, biologists focus on one species or environment. For example, marine biologists study ocean life. Ornithologists study birds, entomologists explore the insect world, and botanists deal with plants. Biologists make small changes to the environment, a plant, or an animal so they can observe how it is affected by these changes. A microscope is one of a biologist's most useful tools. They also use computers to help them analyze the results of experiments.

Young Scientists at Work

Acid rain is rain polluted with man-made chemicals. How does acid rain affect plants in an ecosystem?

Materials:

Two spray bottles

One measuring cup

Distilled water

1 cup (240 milliliters) vinegar

Adhesive labels

Two small, healthy plants of the same size and species

Instructions:

1. Fill one spray bottle with distilled water, and label it "water."

2. Pour 1 cup (240 ml) each of distilled water and vinegar into the other spray bottle. Label it "acid rain."

3. Label one plant "water" and the other "acid rain." Place them in a warm, sunny window.

4. Every day for three weeks, spray the plant leaves, and keep the soil moist. Use only the water spray bottle on the water plant, and only the acid rain spray bottle on the acid rain plant.

Observations:

What differences do you see between the two plants?

How might acid rain affect a different ecosystem, such as a field of corn?

Your home is a type of ecosystem. Your family is a community of living things depending on each other. Some members work for money to buy food for all to eat. Your house is an artificial environment, but it is still your habitat. It may be easy to forget that you are part of nature. If you take a look around your home, you will find clues about how you and your family fit into a larger ecosystem.

What makes your house a comfortable environment? Do you depend on plants or animals for shelter, warmth, or protection?

Look into the refrigerator. Do you see food items that come from nature? Can you think of food chains that include you?

Turn on the tap of the sink faucet. What part do you play in the water cycle? Do you know where the water you drink comes from? Where does the water go after your family uses it?

Look in your room. Did any of your furniture come from nature? What about your clothes? Which items are made from artificial materials?

Key Words

aquatic: water environments

artificial: man made

biodiversity: the variety of different species of plants and animals in an environment

coniferous: type of tree that produces cones

deciduous: type of tree with leaves that fall off each year

elevation: the height of a location above sea level

extinct: no longer existing on Earth

fossil fuels: fuels that come from the ancient remains of plants and animals

genetic material: chemicals in a cell that determine the traits passed from parents to offspring

habitat: the natural environment of an organism

invertebrates: animals that have no backbone

microorganism: any living thing that is so small it can only be seen using a microscope

natural resources: materials supplied by nature

niche: a unique place occupied by a species in its habitat

organisms: living things

pollinate: fertilize

species: organisms of the same or similar kind that can breed together to produce offspring that can also breed

Index

Log on to www.av2books.com

AV² by Weigl brings you media enhanced books that support active learning. Go to www.av2books.com, and enter the special code found on page 2 of this book. You will gain access to enriched and enhanced content that supplements and complements this book. Content includes video, audio, weblinks, quizzes, a slide show, and activities.

AV² Online Navigation

Book Pages
AV² pages directly correspond to pages in the book.

Audio
Listen to sections of the book read aloud.

Video
Watch informative video clips.

Embedded Weblinks
Gain additional information for research.

Try This!
Complete activities and hands-on experiments.

Key Words
Study vocabulary, and complete a matching word activity.

Quizzes
Test your knowledge.

Slide Show
View images and captions, and prepare a presentation.

AV² was built to bridge the gap between print and digital. We encourage you to tell us what you like and what you want to see in the future.

Sign up to be an AV² Ambassador at www.av2books.com/ambassador.